Snowman
Sniffles

N. M. Bodecker

Snowman
Sniffles

And Other Verse

ILLUSTRATED BY THE AUTHOR

A Margaret K. McElderry Book

ATHENEUM   1983   NEW YORK

LIBRARY OF CONGRESS CATALOGING IN PUBLICATION DATA

Bodecker, N. M.
Snowman Sniffles and other verse.
"A Margaret K. McElderry book."
Summary: A collection of light and humorous poems.
1. Children's poetry, American. [1. Humorous poetry.
2. American poetry] I. Title.
PS3552.O33S6 1983 811'.54 82–13927
ISBN 0–689–50263–X

Published simultaneously in Canada by McClelland & Stewart, Ltd.
Composition by Maryland Linotype, Baltimore, Maryland.
Printed and bound by Halliday Lithograph Company, Inc.
West Hanover, Massachusetts   First Edition

A SPARROW IN WINTER

The summer birds
have come and gone
and, in the early
winter sun,

a sparrow pecks
the frozen ground,
but stops to make
a cheerful sound,

as if of all
the birds there be
he'd be himself
most cheerfully.

SNOWMAN SNIFFLES

At winter's end
a snowman grows
a snowdrop
on his carrot nose,

a little, sad,
late-season sniff
dried by the spring
wind's handkerchief.

But day and night
the sniffles drop
like flower buds
—they never stop,

until you wake
and find one day
the cold, old man
has run away,

and winter's winds
that blow and pass
left drifts of snowdrops
in the grass,

reminding us:
where such things grow
a snowman sniffed
not long ago.

RUTH LUCE AND
BRUCE BOOTH

Said little Ruth Luce
to little Bruce Booth:
"Lithen," said Ruth
"I've a little looth tooth!"

Said little Bruce Booth:
"Tho what if you do?
that'th nothing thpethial—
I've a looth tooth too!"

HARRY PERRY
BOYSONBERRY

Harry Perry Boysonberry
never thought that he would marry,
married Mary Carey who
said to Harry's mom: "I do
for some reason want to marry
Harry Perry Boysonberry."

I'M NEVER AS GOOD
AS I WANT TO BE

I'm never as good as I want to be,
and sometimes too bad when I'm bad,
and always a little bit silly
—or so says my serious dad.

I'm terribly fond of my daddy,
and proud of him as can be,
so isn't *he* just a *bit* silly,
not to be proud of *me*?

CATS AND DOGS

Some like cats, and some like dogs,
and both of course are nice
if cats and dogs are what you want
—but I myself like mice.

For dogs chase cats, and cats chase rats
—I guess they think it's fun.
I like my mouse the most because
he won't chase anyone.

MY TROUBLE WITH PORRINGERS
AND ORANGES

I had a pewter
porringer
in which I kept
my oranger,

I mean I kept
my orange
in my pewter
porringe.

I couldn't ever
make them rhyme,
though I kept trying
all the time;

and that is what
my trouble is
with porringers
and oranges.

BEWARE OF DOG!

Beware of dog!
Beware of cat!
Beware of rat
and mouse!
Beware of bat,
and bee,
and gnat,
and flea,
and fly,
and louse

—and anybody else
who may
be guarding this guy's house!

BLACK-EYED SUSAN

Black-eyed Susan,
Lazy Susan,
Susan what's the matter?
Do you want
your breakfast served
on a revolving platter?

ALICIA PATRICIA

Alicia
Patricia,
known
as Trish,
was
too deliciously
ticklish;

at even
the ghost
of a hint
of a wink,
Alicia
Patricia
was tickled
pink.

ORDER

In Waterbury berries grow
neatly, nicely in a row.

All but one—it left the border!

—but was quickly called to order.

Oh, that worrisome and very
wicked Waterbury berry.

A ZOO WITHOUT BARS

Whale

The whale can swallow
a thousand sardines;
he is the biggest
of fish soup tureens.

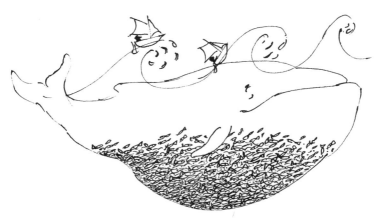

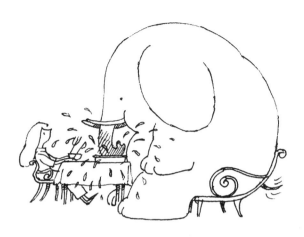

Elephant

If you are
an elephant
you need not
be too elegant.

But *I* think
it is gross
—eating with
your nose.

Giraffe

I like
giraffe
and hope that he
in his
own way
is fond of me,

despite
the fact
that he and I
did never
quite
see eye to eye.

Camel

The camel is
a little
grumpy.

You would be too
if you were
lumpy.

Rooster

The rooster's
crowing
in the morning
is just his
silly way
of yawning.

Cockatoo

The cockatoo
will say to you
what you say to
the cockatoo:

"Good boy," say you;
"Good boy," says he.
And there you are,
and there he be.

A day with him
is nicely spent;
he never starts
an argument.

Lamb

In Noah's
ark
a little lamb
said: "Noah,
tell me
who I am.
My mom is 'sheep.'
My dad is 'ram.'
Now please, sir,
tell me
who I am."

Crocodile

I trust you not,
O crocodile,
and know not if
you yawn or smile.

But smile or yawn
your teeth look vile
—how could I trust
that crocosmile?

Hedgehog

The hedgehog
is a prickly
fellow,
but inside
he is soft
and mellow.

Chipmunk

The chipmunk,
when she stuffs
her cheeks,
could carry food
for weeks
and weeks.

But I should think
that sort of
storage
would turn her stores
to gruel
and porridge.

Chameleon

"Silly!"
the chameleon
said.
"When *you* blush,
you just turn *red*.

"*I*
am such
a clever fellow
I can blush
both *green* and *yellow*!"

Frog

The frog,
when he's alone
and sad,
writes poems
on
his lily pad:

*Froggies are green
bluefish are blue,
guppies are sweet,
and so are you.*

Lion

The lion,
when he roars
at night,
gives many people
quite
a fright!

The lion,
when he roars
by day,
scares people near him
far
away.

And when
he sleeps,
his lion snore
is quite as scary as
his
roar.

Hippopotamus

The hippopotamus—
how odd—
loves rolling
in the river mud.

It makes him
neither hale nor ruddy,
just lovely
hippopotamuddy.

Zebra and Leopard

Zebras want polka dots,
leopards want stripes;
the whole world is nothing
but grumbles and gripes!

Pelican

This little pelican could—

this little pelican can—

this little pelican would,
if it could,
do its pelican-kin's can-can.

Warthog

The warthog
is
no raving
beauty
—but what
of that?
He does
his
duty!

Possum

The possum's tail
is called
prehensile,
and is .
her usefullest
utensil.

Mosquito

A mosquito
from Buckingham Palace
to its Maker
claimed to have been:
By Special Appointment Purveyor
of Mosquito Bites
To the Queen.

Weevil

A weevil
will
what its
wee will
will.

OASES

Oases
are places
in wide, sandy spaces
where date palms
grow dates
while the desert sun
blazes.
They sit there
in sunshine
so bright
that it hurts,

green date-plates
presenting
the desert's
desserts.

DON'T LEAVE THE SPOON
IN THE SYRUP

The lid was off,
the spoon was in,
the syrup smelled deliciously;
I looked,
I watched,
I sniffed,
and then—
I licked it syrupticiously!

BARTHOLOMEW THE HATTER

Bartholomew the hatter
said breakfast made him fatter,
so he sat down to dinner
to eat himself thinner.

But when his breakfast pork was served
did he just once say: "When"?
Not he. He simply sighed: "My dear,
I'm gettin' fat again . . ."

NUT

"Life is peachy!"
sighed a nut
sleeping on
its apri-cot.

RADISH

The radish is
the only dish
that isn't flat
but spherical.

Eating small
green peas off it
could make you quite
hysterical!

WHY DO WEEPING
WILLOWS WEEP?

Why do weeping willows weep?
Wide awake or fast asleep,
morning, noonday, midnight deep,
why do weeping willows weep,

raining, when the song birds flee,
leaves like tears all over me?
I don't know why that should be;
neither does the willow tree.

HIGH-HO, MISTLETOE!

High-ho,
mistletoe!
I'm not hard
to please,
I love
the land
of mists
and sloe
where kisses
grow
on trees,

where dawns
are veils
of bluets' wings,
and days
a haze
of thyme,
and evenings
roads
through down
and dune
where woolly
hare bells
chime.

For there
at noon
the pine trees
keep
still midnight
deep
within,
and in
among
the moving
boughs
the Cheshire kittens
grin.

SMALL RAINS

Bedtime tears
and evening sorrow,
here today
and gone tomorrow.

Small rains that pass
and passing cry:
"How-do-you-do?
Good-by, good-by."

WHEN SKIES ARE LOW
AND DAYS ARE DARK

When skies are low
and days are dark,
and frost bites
like a hungry shark,
when mufflers muffle
ears and nose,
and puffy sparrows
huddle close—
how nice to know
that February
is something purely
temporary.

FOOTPRINTS OF A SPARROW

Footprints of a sparrow
in the new, clean snow.

And there, now, right on top of them,
the scratchings of a crow!

Clearly, and without a doubt,
what the sparrow wrote about
angrily the crow scratched out . . .

would you not like to know
what sort of sparrow silliness
did aggravate that crow?

SPRING GALE

The world is spinning madly,
I can feel the way it scoots,
shaking loose a million, billion
dandelion parachutes.
The birds cling to the maple trees
with little squeaks and hoots;
the maples cling to rocks and earth
for dear life with their roots

—but Dad and I are safe
in our great, big rubber boots.

IN A FIELD OF CLOVER
BY THE RIVER CHARLES

The day
was grey
and full of cloud,
the clover
smelled of honey,
and even when
the rain began
that made the day
seem sunny.

AFTER THE RAINS

After the rains,
when I opened my door
the spiders were at it
as hard as before,

mending their nets,
as the sun came again,
the patient, dependable
fly-fishermen.

MY GIRL MAGGIE

Snaggle-tooth
and twinkle-toe
how deliciously
they grow,
one above
and one below,
who could ever
tell her no?
Oh!
My girl Maggie.

Crinkle-nose
and knobble-knee,
freckle-faced
and fancy free,
all I know that's nice
is she
—but she'll never
marry me.
Fie!
My girl Maggie.

BEDTIME MUMBLE

A cherry pip,
a turnip tip,
a snippet in the snow,
a snail, a rail,
a lobster tail,
the guppy has no toe.

A honeybee,
a money tree,
a day without a sorrow,
a dime, they say,
is here today
and gone again tomorrow.

59

A summer song,
a winter long,
a mumble for your yawning,
"Good-by, good-by!"
the day-birds cry,
"and see you in the morning."

OCTOBER NIGHTS
IN MY CABIN

Acorns drop
on my roof
all night,
each with a hard
little:
"Plonk!"

Raindrops drum
on my roof
all-right
like fingertips
over
my bunk.

Wild geese pass over
my roof
in flight,
the old, grey
travelers
honk!

There's a patter of feet
on my roof
that might
be a squirrel,
or chipmunk,
or skunk . . .

and acorns keep dropping
—or aren't they
quite
acorns, the things
that go:
"Bonk!"

but peanuts dropped
in the pale
moonlight
from a fumble-nosed
elephant's
trunk?

FIRST SNOWFLAKE

Snowflake,
snowflake,
blowing into town
like one, last,
summer's-end
dandelion down,
or a cold little
raindrop
in her winter nightgown.

BUMBLE BEE

I am a bumble bee,
think kindly thoughts of me,
I filled your summer mornings
        with my humming.

Now days are growing short
and I suppose I ought
to stop this evening mumble
        in the clover;

but when I think it's done,
the hum goes on and on,
for no one will believe
                    that winter's coming;

when stillness should begin,
small songs keep dropping in
like raindrops from the trees
                    when rain is over.

INDEX